# BRAIN
# BAFFLERS

## Robert Steinwachs

*Illustrated by Myron Miller*

 **Sterling Publishing Co., Inc.  New York**

**Library of Congress Cataloging-in-Publication Data**
Steinwachs, Robert.
    Brainbafflers / byRobertSteinwachs ; illustratedbyMyron
Miller.
        p.    cm.
    Includes index.
    ISBN 0-8069-8789-8 (Trade)
    ISBN 0-8069-8787-1 (Paper)
    1. Puzzles.   I. Title.
    GV1493.S78   1993
    793.73—dc20                                        92-39352
                                                          CIP


10   9   8   7   6   5   4   3

Published in 1993 by Sterling Publishing Company, Inc.
387 Park Avenue South, New York, N.Y. 10016
© 1993 by Robert Steinwachs
Distributed in Canada by Sterling Publishing
℅ Canadian Manda Group, P.O. Box 920, Station U
Toronto, Ontario, Canada M8Z 5P9
Distributed in Great Britain and Europe by Cassell PLC
Villiers House, 41/47 Strand, London WC2N 5JE, England
Distributed in Australia by Capricorn Link Ltd
P.O. Box 665, Lane Cove, NSW 2066
*Manufactured in the United States of America*
*All rights reserved*

Sterling ISBN 0-8069-8789-8 (Trade)
        ISBN 0-8069-8787-1 (Paper)

The author claims neither to have originated nor improved upon a good portion of these puzzles. The puzzles were collected over many years through verbal exchange, mimeographed, photocopied, or hand-scrawled on paper. The author's intent was to preserve for other enthusiasts some very informative and entertaining puzzles which might otherwise be lost forever. Were it possible to validate originality, the author would gladly give credit to those who created any of the puzzles listed.

Edited by Marie Steinwachs. Additional support from Julia Steinwachs, Christine Steinwachs, Marie Steinwachs, Marsha Boone, Louise Stark, Anne Padelford, and Michael Hartley. Graphics by Linda Moore and Bruce R. Helm.

# CONTENTS

# INTRODUCTION

OUT OF SEVERAL IMPOSSIBLE TO FIND THE
HUNDRED PUZZLES ORIGIN OF EACH ONE. THEY
COLLECTED IN THE ARE ASSEMBLED FOR YOUR
PAST FIFTY PLEASURE AND ARE NOT ALL

YEARS THESE ARE NONSENSICAL, BUT TOUCH
THE ONES WE HAVE ON MATHEMATICS, HISTORY,
NOT BEEN ABLE TO GEOGRAPHY, ENGLISH, LOGIC
FIND PUBLISHED PROBLEMS AND BIBLE KNOW-

ANYWHERE. THEY LEDGE. SEE HOW MANY
ARE THE TYPE OF YOU CAN SOLVE WITHOUT
PUZZLES THAT MAKE REFERRING TO THE BACK
THEIR APPEARANCE IN ANSWER PAGES. BE
THE FORM OF COPIED CAREFUL! SOME MAY BE
SHEETS IN OFFICES, PURPOSELY TRICKY AND
STORES, SCHOOLS, AND MISLEADING TO YOU,
CLUBS. IT WOULD BE, BUT VERY OFTEN, ARE
AFTER ALL THESE YEARS, MOST INFORMATIVE.

GOOD LUCK! **(Solution on page 77)**

# Warm Up on a Few Easy Ones

1. How many apples would you have if you took two apples from three apples? **(Solution on page 80)**

2. How many of each kind of animal did Moses take on the Ark? **(Solution on page 84)**

3. If a billion follows a million and a trillion follows a billion, what number follows a trillion?
**(Solution on page 87)**

4. Gus and Joe are raising pigs. Gus said that if Joe would give him two pigs they would have an equal number, but if Gus gave Joe two of his, Joe would have twice as many as Gus. How many pigs did they each have?
   **(Solution on page 85)**

5. How many months have twenty-eight days?
   **(Solution on page 85)**

6. Is it legal for a man to marry his widow's sister?
   **(Solution on page 86)**

7. If you had to swallow one pill every half hour, how much time would it take for you to swallow three pills?
   **(Solution on page 87)**

8. What day would yesterday be if Thursday was four days before the day after tomorrow?
   **(Solution on page 92)**

9. How should you pronounce the second day of the week Tee-use-day or Twos-dee?     **(Solution on page 94)**

10. Counting one number per second twenty-four hours per day, how long would it take to count to a billion? A trillion?     **(Solution on page 92)**

11. Write down the number eleven thousand, eleven hundred, and eleven.     **(Solution on page 90)**

12. What is it you sit on, sleep in, and brush your teeth with?
    **(Solution on page 89)**

13. Write in what every good citizen should do on election day. _ _ _ _     **(Solution on page 88)**

14. If Mama Bull, Papa Bull, and Baby Bull are in the pasture and Baby Bull gets scared, who would he run to? **(Solution on page 86)**

15. Write your name in the spaces provided below.

_____ _____

**(Solution on page 81)**

# Just for Your Information

Let's say you would only gamble with 10% of your money and would win just as many times as you lose. Would you break even?

For example: Start with $100 and gamble with $10. You lose, leaving $90. Now bet 10% ($9) and win. You are left with $99! Or start with $100, gamble with $10, and win, giving you $110. Bet 10% ($11), lose, and you end up again with $99!

16. Unscramble these letters and make one word from them, using all letters once: OERWNDO
    **(Solution on page 88)**

17. Which is better: One raise per year of $2,000 or a raise of $500 every six months for an indefinite time?
    **(Solution on page 93)**

18. Read this aloud and see if you can decipher the conversation:

    Saville der dago
    Toussin buses inaro
    Nojo demis trux
    Summit cousin
    Summit dux
    **(Solution on page 86)**

19. Too easy? Try this one!

    FUNEM?
    SVFM
    FUNEX?
    SVFX
    OKMNX
    **(Solution on page 83)**

20. If you had a piece of paper that was 0.001 inch thick, how tall a pile would it make if it was doubled fifty times? **(Solution on page 88)**

21. Just $1.00 in the bank drawing 10% compound interest for two hundred years would amount to how much? **(Solution on page 90)**

22. At $1.00 a pack of cigarettes, if you quit smoking for fifty years and put the money in a bank account, how much money would you have? Figure 10% interest. **(Solution on page 92)**

23. Two cities are exactly one hundred miles apart. Charlie leaves City A driving at thirty m.p.h. and Joe leaves City B a half an hour later driving sixty m.p.h. Who will be closer to City A when they meet?
**(Solution on page 90)**

24. A man went into a hardware store and priced certain items. He was told they were $0.25 each. He replied, "I would like one hundred, please," and the clerk rang up $0.75 on the register for the entire purchase. What did the man buy?     **(Solution on page 93)**

25. The score of the baseball game is five to four, in favor of the home team. It is the last of the seventh inning and not one man on either side even reached second base. Can you explain why?     **(Solution on page 91)**

26. A poor man can make one cigarette from six butts. How many cigarettes can he make from thirty-six butts?
**(Solution on page 86)**

27. A man walked into a bar in a resort area and said to the bartender, "Water, water." The bartender immediately pulled a gun out from under the bar and shot it. The man said, "Thank you," and left. Why?
**(Solution on page 94)**

28. A man left home one day and made three left turns and met a man with a mask on. What was the first man's profession?     **(Solution on page 94)**

29. A man walked into a restaurant and ordered a bowl of albatross soup. At first taste he shouted, "Oh, no!" and went outside and shot himself. Why?
**(Solution on page 88)**

30. Four people can sit at a table in twenty-four different arrangements. How many arrangements are possible for seating eight people?     **(Solution on page 83)**

31. Name ten cities starting with the letter "M" which have over a million people living in them, *only one city per country.*     **(Solution on page 81)**

32. Name twenty-eight parts of the body which are spelled with four letters. *No slang, abbreviations, or plurals allowed.*
**(Solution on page 77)**

33. Which number follows ten thousand ninety-five?
Ten thousand ninety-seven?
Ten thousand ninety-nine?
**(Solution on page 79)**

34. Without using the dictionary, how is "polop-ony" pronounced? **(Solution on page 77)**

35. In the spaces in the box, place the numbers 1 through 16 without any consecutive number touching.
**(Solution on page 84)**

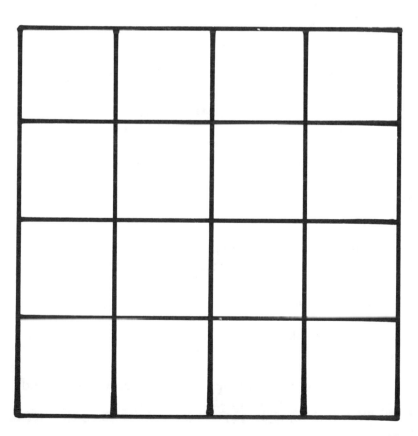

36. A man can paint a room in four hours, and another man can paint the same room in two hours. How long would it take to paint the room if they worked together? **(Solution on page 87)**

37. Can you make four equilateral triangles with six toothpicks? **(Solution on page 87)**

38. A dog had three puppies, named Mopsy, Topsy and Spot. What was the mother's name. **(Solution on page 94)**

39. A microbe doubles itself every second, and in one minute it fills a jar. How long would it take to fill the same jar if you started with four microbes?
    **(Solution on page 92)**

40. A boy and a girl born on the same day of the same year with the same parents are not twins. How is this possible? **(Solution on page 91)**

41. Divide twenty by one-half and add three. What is your answer? **(Solution on page 90)**

42. It is a scientific fact that a person eats over an inch of dirt at every meal. How is this possible?
    **(Solution on page 89)**

| 1 | 2 | 3 | 4 |
|---|---|---|---|
| 2 |   |   |   |
| 3 |   |   |   |
| 4 |   |   |   |

43. **Across**
   1) What dogs do
   2) What fish do
   3) What you do when you eat
   4) What you'll want to do when you solve this

**Down**
   1) Insects
   2) Optical organs
   3) Pester
   4) Comfort     **(Solution on page 87)**

44. Five men checked into a hotel with a bag of peanuts and a monkey. They planned on dividing the peanuts evenly the following morning. However, during the night, one of the men got up, divided the peanuts into five equal parts, took his fifth and had one leftover peanut which he gave to the monkey. He put the other shares of peanuts back into the bag and returned to bed.

A little later, a second man (who did not know that the first man had been up) divided the peanuts five ways and took his fifth. He also had one peanut left over, which he gave to the monkey, and he returned the rest of the peanuts to the bag.

Likewise, during the night the third, fourth and fifth men got up and divided the peanuts, and each had one left over for the monkey. The next morning they divided the remaining peanuts equally five ways. How many peanuts were originally in the bag?

**(Solution on page 84)**

45. Suppose the men followed the same procedure as in Puzzle 44, but had one peanut left for the monkey the following morning. What would be the least number of peanuts they could have started with?

**(Solution on page 85)**

46. In a small midwestern town, the school chimney (approximately 75 feet tall) needed repairs on the top. There was no inside or outside ladder, so the estimates were very high since a contractor would have to build expensive scaffolds.

On the morning after Halloween, the school officials found that someone had put a hay wagon atop the chimney during the night. There was no room for cranes, and helicopters would have been heard. How did the wagon get there? **(Solution on page 81)**

47. What is the least number of queens that could be used to command an entire chessboard?
**(Solution on page 86)**

48. Is the Great Wall of China ten miles long? One hundred miles long? A thousand miles long? Two thousand miles? More? **(Solution on page 89)**

49. Will and Jim were practising shooting, and each scored seventy-five hits out of a hundred. After a little break, Will tried again and hit thirty-five out of fifty shots. Jim did not do any more shooting. Who had the best average for the day?   **(Solution on page 91)**

50. Two half-mile sections of steel railroad track were laid and absolutely secured on each end. The sun expands the steel one foot (12 inches91). Now the overall length is 5,281 feet, and since it is secured at the ends it will buckle in the middle. How high from the ground will it buckle?   **(Solution on page 91)**

51. \_\_ \_\_ \_\_ ERGRO \_\_ \_\_ \_\_

    If you use the same three letters in the same order before and after the given letters, you will get a very dirty word! What is the word?   **(Solution on page 86)**

52. A pipe can fill a tank with water in thirty minutes. A larger pipe can fill the tank in twenty minutes, and still a larger pipe can fill it in ten minutes. How long would it take to fill the tank if all three were opened at once?
    **(Solution on page 85)**

53. To open the safe shown below, certain letters on the three dials must be turned to the arrows. To make the combination easy to remember, it was designed so that the letters on the dials would spell a three-letter English word. What is the word that opens the safe?

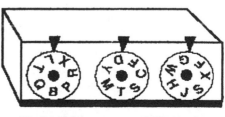

**Letters used**
**1st dial:** QBPRXLT
**2nd dial:** MTSCFDY
**3rd dial:** HJSXFGW   **(Solution on page 88)**

54. A young lady looked at a picture and said, "This person's mother was my mother's mother-in-law." Who was in the picture?   **(Solution on page 85)**

55. We asked the stationmaster how long the train would be in the station. He answered, "222222." We also asked about the train on the next track and he answered, "2222222." What did he mean?
**(Solution on page 87)**

56. A four-inch cube of solid-white material is painted black on all six faces, and then cut into one-inch cubes. Some of the small cubes will have three black faces, some will have two black faces, some one, and some none. How many will there be of each?
**(Solution on page 91)**

57. GHOTI

Broken down phonetically, the above word will be pronounced "FISH." How? **(Solution on page 94)**

58. How many spaces in a wheel with 16 spokes—15, 16, or 17? **(Solution on page 93)**

59. Three playing cards are in a row. A diamond is to the left of a spade (not necessarily next to it). An eight is to the right of a king. A ten is to the left of a heart. A heart is to the left of a spade. What are the three cards? **(Solution on page 93)**

60. If you drove somewhere averaging 60 m.p.h. and you returned the same distance averaging 40 m.p.h., what would your average speed be?
**(Solution on page 92)**

61. If your peacock laid an egg just six inches across your neighbor's property line, who would legally own the egg?    **(Solution on page 90)**

62. Read the sentence below:

JULY 4TH, THE DAY OF THE
ADOPTION OF THE DECLARATION
OF INDEPENDENCE, IS CELEBRATED IN
ALL OF THE STATES AND TERRITORIES
OF THE UNITED STATES OF AMERICA.

Now, go back and count the number of times the letter "E" appears in the sentence. Count them only once and do not go back and count them again. How many "E"s did you count?   **(Solution on page 89)**

63. The Sheriff and his posse, while looking for some outlaws in the woods, came upon what they thought were old Indian signs. Can you read them?
**(Solution on page 88)**

64. Fill in the numbers:
Just sure as _____ and _____ are _____
The _____ Wonders of the World
Friday the _____   **(Solution on page 80)**

65. All answers end with "sting."
A sting that cures fatigue
A sting that cures hunger
A sting that tidies your room
A sting that makes you laugh
A sting that cooks your meat
A sting that spoils your tools
A sting that makes you read a book through
A sting that some observe in Lent
A sting that cooks are always using
A sting that browns your bread
**(Solution on page 78)**

66. Rearrange these numbers so they total 34 horizontally, vertically, and diagonally.

| 14 | 6 | 8 | 11 |
|----|----|----|----|
| 16 | 3 | 9 | 5 |
| 12 | 4 | 7 | 2 |
| 10 | 13 | 1 | 15 |

**(Solution on page 79)**

67. If you do the following exercise correctly, you will change the name of an American president into the name of a European country. Check your method, speed and accuracy in following directions.

Write the words GEORGE WASHINGTON.

Take out all the "E"s.

Counting only the remaining letters, add an "L" after each seventh letter. Move the second "G" to the beginning and put the last letter in its place. Whenever three consonants appear together, change their order so that the first consonant in the group becomes the last, the one in the second place takes the first position, and the one in the third position becomes the middle consonant of the group. Take out the last two vowels. Where a double consonant appears, take out both letters. Beginning with the third letter from the left, interchange each two letters. Take out the last two letters. Move the last letter so it will be the first letter. Add a "D" after each fourth letter and at the beginning. Replace every "S" with an "N". Take out the middle three letters. Take out the final letter and put the first letter in its place.

You should now have the name of the European country. **(Solution on page 87)**

68. Twenty-one birds are nesting in a tree. If a man shot into the tree and killed one-seventh of them, how many would remain? **(Solution on page 85)**

69. Name the offspring of:
    Mr. & Mrs. Voyant
    Mr. & Mrs. Tress
    Mr. & Mrs. Nasium
    Mr. & Mrs. Tate
    Mr. & Mrs. Fi
    Mr. & Mrs. Itosis
    Mr. & Mrs. Anthemum
    Mr. & Mrs. Mander
    Mr. & Mrs. Mite     **(Solution on page 83)**

70. Answer the following with parts of the body (no slang).
    **Example:** Heard in Congress while voting **Answer:** eyes
    & nose
    A strong box
    Two baby cows
    A shellfish
    Two measures
    Two places of worship
    Scholars
    Part of a shoe
    What every builder must have
    Something made by whips
    What the soldier carries        **(Solution on page 84)**

71. There are three sealed envelopes. One contains two $5
    bills, one contains a $10 and a $5 bill, and the third
    contains two $10 bills. Unfortunately, all three envelopes
    have the wrong amount marked on the outside. How
    could you correct all three by opening one envelope and
    looking at only one bill?        **(Solution on page 80)**

# Can You Decipher These Famous Nursery Rhymes and Fables?

72. A female of the *Homo sapiens* species was the possessor of a small immature ruminant of the genus Ovis, whose outermost covering reflected all wavelengths of visible light with a luminosity equal to that of a mass of naturally occurring microscopically crystalline water. Regardless of the translational pathway chosen by the *Homo sapiens* female, there was a 100% probability that the aforementioned ruminant would select the same pathway. **(Solution on page 93)**

73. A research team proceeded toward the apex of a natural geologic protuberance, the purpose of their expedition being the procurement of a sample of fluid hydride of oxygen in a large vessel, the exact size of which was unspecified. One member of the team precipitously descended, sustaining severe damage to the upper cranial portion of his anatomical structure; subsequently the second member of the team performed a self-rotational translation oriented in the direction taken by the first team member. **(Solution on page 89)**

74. A young male human was situated near the intersection of two supporting elements at right angles to each other; said subject was involved in ingesting a saccharine composition prepared in conjunction with the ritual observance of an annual fixed-day religious festival. Insertion into the saccharine composition of the opposable digit of his forelimb was followed by removal of a drop of genus Prunus. Subsequently, the subject made a declarative statement regarding the high quality of his character as a young male human. **(Solution on page 94)**

75. A geriatric human female proceeded to a storage compartment for the purpose of procuring a fragment of osseous tissue from an unidentified deceased specimen to transfer to an indigent carnivorous domesticated mammal, *Canis familiaris*, family Canidae. Upon arrival at her destination, she found the storage compartment in denuded condition, with the consequence that the indigent carnivore was deprived of the intended donation. **(Solution on page 94)**

76. A human female, extremely captious and given to opposed behavior, was questioned as to the dynamic state of her cultivated tract of land used for the production of various types of flora. The tract components were enumerated as argentous tone-producing agents, a rare

species of oceanic growth, and pulchritudinous young females situated in a linear orientation.
**(Solution on page 93)**

77. Complications arose during an investigation of dietary influence; one researcher was unable to assimilate adipose tissue, and another was unable to consume tissue consisting chiefly of muscle fibre. By a reciprocal arrangement between the two researchers, total consumption of the viands under consideration was achieved, thus leaving the original container of the viands devoid of contents.    **(Solution on page 91)**

78. A triumvirate of murine rodents totally devoid of ophthalmic acuity was observed in a state of rapid locomotion in pursuit of an agriculturalist's uxorial adjunct. Said adjunct then performed a triple caudectomy utilizing an acutely honed bladed instrument generally used for subdivision of edible tissue.
**(Solution on page 91)**

For more eccentric equations, see pages 35–41.

# Can You Decipher These Famous Sayings?

79. A mass of concentrated earthly material perennially rotating on its axis will not accumulate an accretion of bryophytic vegetation.   **(Solution on page 90)**

80. A superabundance of talent skilled in the preparation of gastronomic concoctions will impair the quality of a certain potable solution made by immersing a gallinaceous bird in ebullient Adam's ale.
**(Solution on page 86)**

81. Individuals who perforce are constrained to be domiciled in vitreous structures of patent frangibility should on no account employ petrous formations as projectiles.
**(Solution on page 85)**

82. That prudent avis which matutinally deserts the coziness of its abode will ensnare a vermiculate creature.
**(Solution on page 88)**

83. Everything that coruscates with effulgence is not ipso facto aurous.   **(Solution on page 92)**

84. Do not dissipate your competence by hebetudinous prodigality lest you subsequently lament an exiguous inadequacy.   **(Solution on page 94)**

85. An addlepate and his specie divaricate with startling prematurity.   **(Solution on page 94)**

86. It can be no other than a maleficent horizontally pro-
pelled current of gaseous matter whose portentous ad-
vent is not the harbinger of a modicum of beneficence.
**(Solution on page 89)**

87. Scintillate, scintillate, globule of vivific
Fain would I fathom thy nature specific
Loftily poised above the capacious
Closest resembling a gem carbonaceous.
**(Solution on page 91)**

# Eccentric Equations

See how many of these equations you can solve without looking up the answers. The first one is free!

88. 26=L of the A    **(Solution: Letters of the Alphabet)**

89. 7=W of the A W    **(Solution on page 93)**

90. 10=C    **(Solution on page 78)**

91. 1,001=A N    **(Solution on page 79)**

92. 12=S of the Z    **(Solution on page 80)**

93. 54=C in a D (with the J)     **(Solution on page 81)**

94. 9=P in the S S     **(Solution on page 81)**

95. 88=P K     **(Solution on page 89)**

96. 32=D F at which W F     **(Solution on page 95)**

97. 18=H in a G C     **(Solution on page 94)**

98. 90=D in a R A     **(Solution on page 93)**

99. 200=D for P G in M     **(Solution on page 92)**

100. 8=S on a S S     **(Solution on page 91)**

101. 3=B M (S II T R)  **(Solution on page 90)**

102. 24=H in a D  **(Solution on page 89)**

103. 1=W on a U  **(Solution on page 86)**

104. 1,000=W that a P is W  **(Solution on page 91)**

105. 29=D in F in a L Y  **(Solution on page 93)**

106. 64=S on a C B  **(Solution on page 81)**

107. 40=D and N of the G F  **(Solution on page 82)**

108. 6=W of H the E  **(Solution on page 108)**

109. 101=D     **(Solution on page 89)**

110. 60=S in a M     **(Solution on page 95)**

111. 7=H of R     **(Solution on page 95)**

112. 5=F on each H (or T on each F)
**(Solution on page 93)**

113. 40=T with A B     **(Solution on page 91)**

114. 30=D H S A J and N     **(Solution on page 88)**

115. 1=D at a T     **(Solution on page 85)**

116. 2=T D (and a P in a P T)
    **(Solution on page 85)**

117. 4=H of the A     **(Solution on page 86)**

118. 13=C in a S     **(Solution on page 87)**

119. 8=P of S in the E L     **(Solution on page 90)**

120. 20,000=L U the S     **(Solution on page 90)**

121. 360=D in a C     **(Solution on page 86)**

122. 60=M in an H     **(Solution on page 94)**

123. 13=B D     **(Solution on page 94)**

124. 2001=A S O     **(Solution on page 93)**

125. 6=S on a C     **(Solution on page 91)**

126. 32=T including W T     **(Solution on page 91)**

127. 100=L on a C     **(Solution on page 88)**

128. 3=W M     **(Solution on page 87)**

129. 7=D     **(Solution on page 80)**

130. 1, 2=B M S     **(Solution on page 88)**

131. 206=B in the B     **(Solution on page 88)**

132. 6=S on a H     **(Solution on page 91)**

133. 4=S in a Y     **(Solution on page 93)**

134. 2=Y before the M     **(Solution on page 94)**

135. 21=G S     **(Solution on page 93)**

136. 4=C in a C C     **(Solution on page 91)**

For more eccentric equations, see pages 35–41.

# The Delivery Route

137. The driver of a beer delivery truck had to make deliveries
to nine stores in nine different towns—K,I,F,
G,E,N,M,L, and J. He did not want to go over the same
route twice and he did not want to go to any of the nine
towns more than once. From the map above, list the towns
in the order he should make his deliveries. The brewery
is town P.    **(Solution on page 85)**

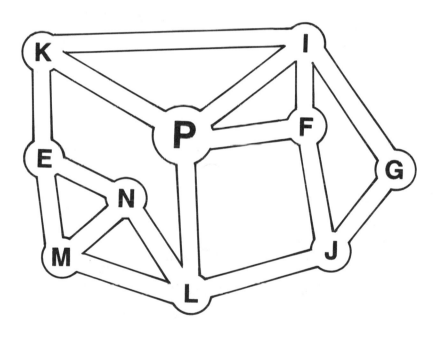

138. How many letters are there in the Hawaiian alphabet?
**(Solution on page 86)**

139. How could you take one from nineteen and leave
twenty?    **(Solution on page 87)**

140. Three men were selling melons at $1.00 each at a market. One started with 33 melons, the second with 29 melons, and the third man with only 27. They each sold only a few until one man dropped his price to 3/$1.00. The other two did likewise, and at this price they all soon sold out. Comparing their business later, they found that each took in the same amount of money. How did this happen?  **(Solution on page 88)**

141. A boy was offered a bonus if he sold one hundred subscriptions to a magazine. Each day he sold three subscriptions more than he had on the previous day, and on the eighth day he reached his one hundred quota. How many subscriptions did he sell each day?
**(Solution on page 90)**

SO, WHAT WAS YOUR BONUS FOR SELLING 100 SUBSCRIPTIONS?

PONY CHOW

# Silly Sequences

142. 1 2 5 10 13 26 29? **(Solution on page 90)**

143. 9 7 8 5 7 3? **(Solution on page 88)**

# Petals Around the Rose

144.

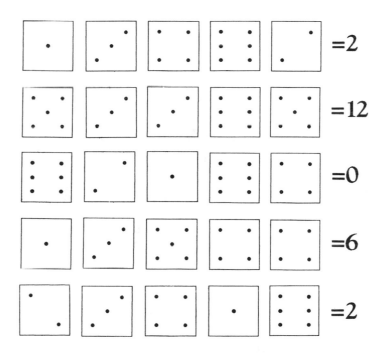

Study the above samples and see if you can break the code. **(Solution on page 85)**

145. How many holes are there in a "Chinese Checkers" board?    **(Solution on page 88)**

146. In which war did the first jet airplane combat take place? **(Solution on page 87)**

147. Which bird can swim but can't fly? **(Solution on page 95)**

148. Which gambling device was invented around 1244 B.C.E.? **(Solution on page 87)**

149. On which day does Mardi Gras begin? **(Solution on page 86)**

150. What percentage of the circle is labelled A and what percentage is labelled B?    **(Solution on page 93)**

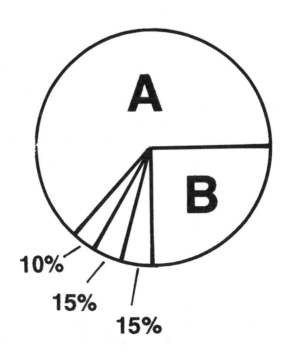

151. Which word has three pairs of letters?
     **(Solution on page 90)**

152. What is 550 foot lbs. per second equal to?
     **(Solution on page 90)**

153. What color is traditional for a Chinese wedding dress?
     **(Solution on page 94)**

154. Which country had the first adhesive postage stamp?
     **(Solution on page 94)**

47

155. Multiply the number of letters in the sign of the lion by the number of letters in the sign of the bull. Subtract the number of letters in the sign of the fish. Divide by the number of letters in the sign of the crab. Multiply by the number of letters in the sign of the twins. What is the answer? **(Solution on page 93)**

156. Tom is older than Sue, and Sue is younger than Mary, who is older than Tom. Who is the oldest of the three? **(Solution on page 92)**

157. You buy a large bottle of juice in a returnable bottle for $1.60. The juice costs $1.20 more than the bottle. After the bottle is empty, you return it for your refund. How much should you receive? **(Solution on page 89)**

158. In grid A below, the circles have been placed so that no circle is in the same row or in the same column as any other circle. However, two circles are on the same diagonal (the one shown with the arrow). Place four circles on grid B so that no circles are in the same row, column, or diagonal. **(Solution on page 95)**

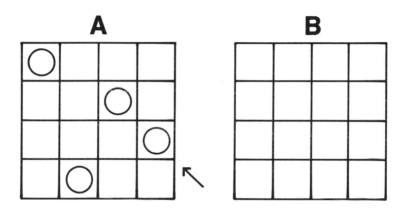

159. Arrange twenty cubes in four piles using these clues:
- All piles contain an even number of cubes.
- There are twice as many cubes in the first pile as in the second pile.
- The largest number of cubes is in the first pile.
- All piles have a different number of cubes.
- Each pile has at least one cube.

How many cubes would be in Pile 1? Pile 2? Pile 3? Pile 4? **(Solution on page 85)**

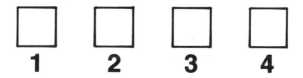

160. Alex played a game of darts. He made five throws and hit the target each time. His total score was sixty points. Where on the target did his darts land?
**(Solution on page 88)**

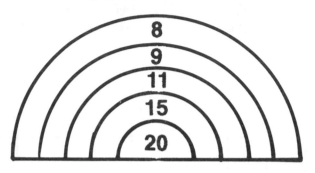

161. In order to win this game of darts, you have to throw four darts and get exactly twenty-six points. Which areas of the board would you hit to get your twenty-six points? If you needed twenty-nine points with four throws, what would you need to hit?    **(Solution on page 91)**

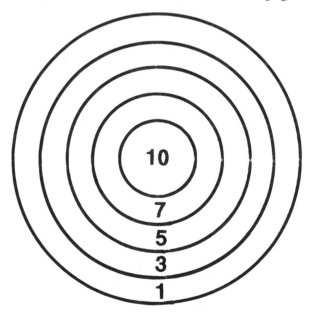

162. How many shots are necessary to score exactly 100 on the target below?     **(Solution on page 92)**

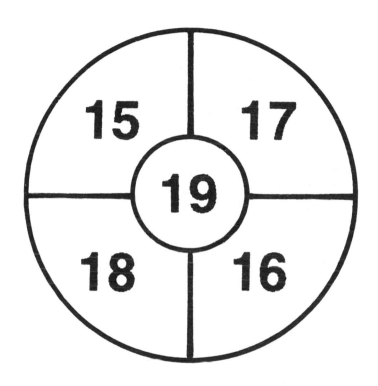

163. September 9, 1981 (9/9/81) was the last time in this century that the product of the month times the day is the last two digits of the year. When will this happen again?
**(Solution on page 92)**

164. In the land of Woz, each person has only one car. The license plate of each car is different, and contains just one letter and one one-digit number including zero. How many people live in the land of Woz?
**(Solution on page 77)**

165. Answer this one quickly. After a gas tank of a car is filled, which happens first?
A. the tank is ¾ empty
B. the tank is ⅔ full    **(Solution on page 89)**

166. A typical license plate is composed of three letters and three numbers (ex. ABC-123) How many of these plates can be made without duplication? How many license plates can be formed if duplication of letters or numbers is not allowed?    **(Solution on page 94)**

167. A man took a truckload of chickens to market. In the first hour he sold one-half of his birds plus one-half of a chicken. The next hour he sold one-third of a chicken. The third hour he sold one-fourth of what he had left plus three-fourths of a chicken. The last hour he sold one-fifth of the chickens plus one-fifth of a chicken. He did not cut up any chickens to make any of these sales. He returned home with nineteen chickens. How many did he take to market? **(Solution on page 94)**

168. What beast of burden can carry more on its back than an elephant? **(Solution on page 90)**

169. In a small town, it was found that ninety percent of the people drank coffee, and eighty percent drank tea. Also, seventy percent drank Bourbon whiskey, and sixty percent drank vodka. None of the people drank all four items, but they all did drink three of the four beverages. What percent of the people drank liquor?
**(Solution on page 92)**

170. A man is twenty years old plus half his age. How old is he?  **(Solution on page 86)**

171. Name thirty parts of the body spelled with five letters. No plurals, no abbreviations, and no slang.
**(Solution on page 83)**

172. A very thrifty housewife was checking soap prices in a supermarket. She noted that brand A was 50% more expensive than brand C and contained 20% less weight than brand B. However, brand B was 50% heavier than brand C, and cost 25% more than brand A. Which would be the best buy?  **(Solution on page 80)**

173. Sam raced Jake on a 100-yard dash, and beat him by 10 yards. The next day Sam told Jake to take a 10-yard lead and they would race again. If they both maintained the same speed as the previous day, would the race be a tie or who would win, and why?  **(Solution on page 85)**

174. Cut a wheel of cheese in 16 fairly equal shapes and approximate weights with only four cuts of a knife. Only straight cuts may be used.  **(Solution on page 83)**

175. Which of the following letter designs is not like the other six?

Y E N F H A Z

**(Solution on page 87)**

176. The first day Tony put a new display of apples in his fruit stand, he sold half of them and gave two to the local policeman. The next day he removed three bruised apples and sold one-third of the remainder. The third day he ate three, gave two more away, and sold one-fourth of what was left. The last day he sold one-fifth of the remainder, threw five rotten ones away, and had enough left for an average-size apple pie. How many apples did he start with? **(Solution on page 87)**

177. How long would it take a half-mile train going one mile a minute to go through a two-mile tunnel?
**(Solution on page 88)**

178. How many minutes would it be before six o'clock if fifty minutes earlier it had been four times as many minutes after three o'clock?     **(Solution on page 93)**

179. Using the following sequence, where would 13 fit in, and why?

8  11  5  4  9  1  7  6  10  3  12  2

**(Solution on page 89)**

180. Alex, twelve years old, is three times as old as his sister. How old will Alex be when he is twice as old as his sister?
**(Solution on page 94)**

181. Which of the following letters do not fit in the series?

A  D  G  I  J  M  P  S

**(Solution on page 92)**

182. Which of the following numbers do not fit in with the order of the others?

2  3  6  7  8  14  15  30

**(Solution on page 90)**

183. Make a path from start to finish that does not cross itself or cut diagonally and totals 54.
**(Solution on page 95)**

| Start | 7 | 9 | 13 |
|-------|---|---|-----|
| 3 | 5 | 7 | 15 |
| 16 | 4 | 7 | 11 |
| 15 | 1 | 3 | Finish |

184. If a five-hour candle and a six-hour candle were lit at the same time, how much time would elapse before one candle would be five times longer than the other?
**(Solution on page 94)**

185. What number is divisible by any number from two to nine, and will always have one number left for a remainder? Hint: The number is less than 3,000! **(Solution on page 93)**

186. If the car rental agency charges $35.00 per day and $0.45 per mile to rent their cars, how many miles can you drive and still keep the cost under $125.00 per day? **(Solution on page 92)**

187. A salesman is paid a salary of $300.00 plus a 40% commission in sales. How much does he have to sell to make an income of $2,000.00? **(Solution on page 90)**

188. If $3,600.00 was invested at 15% interest compounded daily, how much money would there be in seven years? **(Solution on page 89)**

189. Where is the world's highest chimney, and how tall is it (approximately)? **(Solution on page 86)**

## More Sequences . . .

190. Complete these sequences, if you can!
30   5   1   4   12   ? = 6
7   7   7   4   4   ? = 1
**(Solution on page 86)**

# To Find the Meanings, Think of Music

191. Move hitherwards, the entire assembly of those who are steadfast. **(Solution on page 90)**

192. Ecstasy towards the terrestrial sphere. **(Solution on page 91)**

193. Hush, the celestial messengers produce harmonious sounds. **(Solution on page 91)**

194. Creator, cool it, you kooky cats.
**(Solution on page 91)**

195. O tatterdemalion ebony atmosphere.
**(Solution on page 93)**

196. The thing manifested itself at the onset of a transparent day.   **(Solution on page 94)**

197. Embellish the interior passageways.
**(Solution on page 89)**

198. Tintinnabulation of vacillating pendulums in inverted metallic resonant cups.   **(Solution on page 78)**

199. Hey, minuscule urban area south of Jerusalem.
**(Solution on page 81)**

200. Nocturnal timespan of unbroken quietness.
**(Solution on page 86)**

201. This autocratic troika originates near the ascent of Apollo.   **(Solution on page 86)**

202. The primary carol.   **(Solution on page 88)**

203. Natal celebration devoid of color, rather albino, as in a hallucinatory phenomenon for me.
**(Solution on page 92)**

204. Valentino, the roseate proboscis wapiti.
**(Solution on page 93)**

205. Diminutive masculine master of skin-covered percussionistic cylinders.   **(Solution on page 94)**

206. O nativity conifer.   **(Solution on page 94)**

207. During the time bovine caretakers supervised their charges past midnight. **(Solution on page 77)**

208. What offspring abides thus?
**(Solution on page 91)**

209. Removed in a bovine feeding trough.
**(Solution on page 88)**

210. Expectation of arrival at populated area by mythical, masculine, perennial gift-giver.
**(Solution on page 95)**

211. Geographic state of fantasy during the season of Mother Nature's dormancy. **(Solution on page 89)**

212. Proceed to declare something upon a specific geographical Alpine formation. **(Solution on page 92)**

213. Obese personification fabricated of compressed mounds of minute crystals. **(Solution on page 89)**

214. Jovial yuletide desired for the second person singular or plural by us. **(Solution on page 80)**

215. Thoracic–Squirrel Diet barbecue.
**(Solution on page 79)**

# More Bafflers

216. Charley bought a motorcycle to tour the country with. After two years, it had depreciated to $6,000 and in five years it had a book value of $3,750. What did the motorcycle cost originally, and how long before it would have a book value of $0?     **(Solution on page 87)**

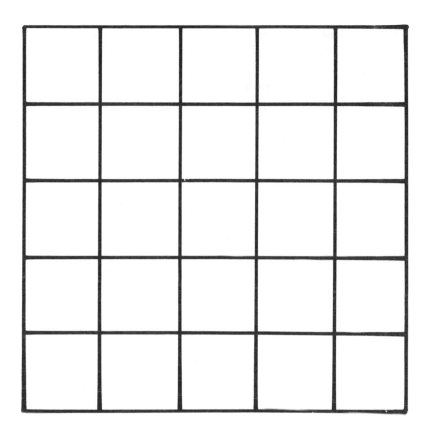

217. Above are twenty-five squares. Take the twenty-six letter alphabet, cross out any one of the letters and fill the squares with the remaining letters. See how many words you can form by joining letters horizontally, vertically, or diagonally. You may go backwards and use a letter in more than one place. By putting the vowels in choice places, the letters were arranged so that I was able to build 104 words. Can you beat that record?

**(Solution on page 81)**

218. One summer, two high school athletes decided to walk 117 miles along a mountain trail. They started out early on Sunday morning packed with energy. However, each day they walked one mile less than they had the previous day. They did not give up, and on the following Monday, eight days later, they finished their hike. How many miles did they hike each day?
**(Solution on page 92)**

219. Why would it take a plane flying from San Francisco to New York nonstop longer than the same type of plane flying from New York to San Francisco, when weather, speed, winds, and all flying conditions were the same each way?     **(Solution on page 88)**

220. Slippery Joe ran against Sneaky Pete, Big Looie the Con, and Dragnet Doug for the mayor's job in a small town. Out of 1,648 total votes, Joe beat Pete by 8 votes, Looie by 76 votes, and Doug by 187 votes. How many votes did each of these stalwart gentlemen receive?
**(Solution on page 87)**

221. Just for fun, how many different ways is the word "shot" used in our modern-day language? I found at least twenty. Can you find more?
**(Solution on page 78)**

222. June 21 has been called the longest day of the year. What day of the year is longer than that day?
**(Solution on page 91)**

223. A bridge was built in a perfect arch across a river. A man walked out on the bridge twenty-seven feet from the shore and determined that the water level of the river was just nine feet below the bridge. When he got to the center of the bridge, he measured again and the distance from the bridge to the water level was ten feet. How wide was the river? **(Solution on page 93)**

224. If you drop one of those "super bounce" rubber balls from a distance of nine feet from the floor, the ball keeps bouncing. Each time it bounces back two-thirds of the distance of the previous bounce. What distance would the ball travel before it stopped?
**(Solution on page 95)**

225. Unscramble the following and, using all the letters, make a ten-letter word that a four-year-old child would recognize. Very possibly you have never had occasion to write the word, but it's likely that you've spoken it several times:

ROAST MULES

**(Solution on page 89)**

226. Replace the letters with numbers in the following addition tasks:

| ABC | LMN | RSTU |
|-----|-----|------|
| + BDE | + ONL | + UTSR |
| FGEB | PQQQ | VWWV |

**(Solution on page 90)**

227. A man drives to work each day averaging a speed of 40 m.p.h. and always arrives just on time to start work. However, one morning the traffic was bad and at the halfway point he found that he was averaging only 20 m.p.h. How fast must he travel the rest of the way to get to work on time? **(Solution on page 86)**

228. If seven cats can catch seven rats seven ways in seven days, how long will it take ten cats to catch ten rats ten ways? **(Solution on page 89)**

229. In his will, a grandfather left each of his grandsons as many dollars as he had grandsons, and each of his granddaughters as many dollars as he had granddaughters. He did likewise with his four great-grandchildren and willed $441 for all. How many grandsons, granddaughters, and great-grandchildren did he have?
**(Solution on page 85)**

230. In which country are the following:
Stonehenge
Alhambra
Parthenon
Eiffel Tower
Colosseum
Piccadilly Circus
Big Ben
Leaning Tower
Blarney Stone
Bridge of Sighs
Black Forest
Kremlin
Matterhorn
Monte Carlo
Little Mermaid
Louvre
Great Pyramid
Mozart's Birthplace
Tivoli Gardens
**(Solutions on page 84)**

# A Good Card Trick

231. Shuffle a deck of cards well, and then spread them face down on the table. Have a friend pick three cards, one at a time. The friend hands you the cards face down without looking at them. You will be able to tell him what each card is and have it written down before you peek at the card! You pick a final card yourself and tell what it is before you look at it. Then turn over all four cards and show that you were right! How is this done? **(Solution on page 79)**

232. A grocery clerk must stack thirty cases of canned vegetables. Each case contains twenty-four cans. He wants to display them in a pyramid, with each row containing one less can than the row below it. Is it possible to use up all the cans and have a top row with only one can? How many rows of cans would he have?
**(Solution on page 91)**

233. Below is an example of a "two-way addition pattern," using the nine digits. The numbers form the correct sum as they stand or rotated 90 degrees to the right. Can you make another similar pattern using the nine digits?
**(Solution on page 95)**

```
  4 8│2
  1 5│7
+ 6 3│9
```

234. My next door neighbor rotated the tires on his car every 5,000 miles. When he had 10,000 miles of use, one of the tires was damaged and replaced. He continued rotating the tires every 5,000 miles but did not use the new tire as a spare until all five tires had worn equally. When the new tire first became a spare, how many miles had he added on his odometer?   **(Solution on page 94)**

235. Suppose a teacher obtains a job with a starting salary of $15,000 and receives a raise of $500 every year for ten years. What will her salary be in ten years? If she was offered the alternative of accepting a 3% raise each year instead of the $500 raise, which would be the higher salary in ten years?   **(Solution on page 92)**

236. More sequences:
    9   7   13   11   17   ?
    57   49   42   36   ?
    5   8   6   9   ?
    1   3   6   10   ?
    1   3   6   11   13   16   18   20   ?
    **(Solutions on page 95)**

237. PART 1769      STONE 49385      PATERSON 17956438
    SO —
    What number should be put in the blank?
    **(Solution on page 90)**

238. If you had $10,000 in the bank and would like it to grow to $20,000 in ten years, what interest would you have to get—assuming annual compounding?
    **(Solution on page 87)**

239. A farmer butchered twenty-pigs in six days. He butchered on every one of the six days and an odd number of pigs each time. How many were butchered on each day?
**(Solution on page 89)**

240. A man wanted to invest exactly $10,000 in five different stocks at the following market price:

202

13

46¼

97½

108

Not taking brokers or any other fees into account, how many of each of the stocks did he buy?
**(Solution on page 87)**

241. A small town, in an effort to raise money, hired a well-known country band to play in its civic stadium. The band offered to give one concert for $10,000 and 20% of the gate receipts. It is assumed that 10,000 people will attend. What admission price would the town have to charge just to break even? What admission price would it have to charge to earn a profit of $25,000? **(Solution on page 85)**

242. Some gentlemen—Sneaky Pete, Looie the Con, and Dragnet Doug—met parolee Bad Bob. Bob told them about a shrine in the Shamir Desert in which there was an idol adorned with jewels. To reach the shrine would take ten days' travel time. A man would need one gallon of water a day to travel and could carry no more than ten

gallons on his back. They each had four two-and-a-half-gallon cans of water with no place available to get more. It would be possible to cache cans of water along the route. They decided to pool their supply and to place it in such places on the route that one man could cross to the shrine and return safely. If a man walked five miles out and returned, he would have no water to leave on the trail. Is it possible to get a man across and return with the loot?     **(Solution on page 80)**

243. A man buys a piece of farm equipment which costs $10,000 and it depreciates 20% of its current value every year. The first year it would depreciate $2,000, the second year $1,600, and so on. How many years would it take for the equipment to reach total depreciation?
**(Solution on page 95)**

244. A farmer took 141 bushels of three different grains to the market and received $565 for the load. His wheat sold for $5 a bushel, corn for $4, and oats for $2.50. How many bushels of each kind of grain did he take to market?     **(Solution on page 83)**

245. If the length and width of a rectangular field totalled 1,350 feet, which figures in length and width would give the most square footage?
**(Solution on page 77)**

246. A    E    HIKLMNOP    UW
   ‾‾‾‾‾‾‾‾‾‾‾‾‾‾‾‾‾‾‾‾‾‾‾‾‾‾‾‾
   BCD    F    J    QRST    V

Does xyz belong above or below the line, and why?
**(Solution on page 90)**

247. Picture a pyramid of blocks. Ten blocks in the bottom row, with one block less in each row for ten rows, totals fifty-five blocks. How many blocks would there be if the pyramid started at one hundred blocks?
**(Solution on page 89)**

248. A man obtained a job in a factory with $20,000 as his starting salary. If he received an 8% raise every year, what would his salary be in ten years?
**(Solution on page 81)**

249. Two planes took off from an airport just thirty minutes apart. The first headed due east, and the second flew due west. In seventy-five minutes they were exactly 700 miles apart. How fast was each plane flying?
**(Solution on page 95)**

250. What is the name of the largest number in the world? If you say a googol, that number has only 100 zeros following the digit. There is a number much larger than this! **(Solution on page 78)**

251. Many years ago, an eccentric woman named Lucy King wrote this riddle. A wealthy manufacturer offered her a prize if she could write a riddle which he could not solve, and her subject was to be from the Bible. Following is Lucy's riddle. Can you solve it?

Adam, God made out of dust,
But thought it best to make me
  first.
So I was made before the man,
To answer God's most holy
  plan.

My body God did make
  complete
But without arms or legs or
  feet.
My ways and acts He did
  control,
But to my body gave no soul.

A living being I became
And Adam gave to me a name.
I from his presence then
  withdrew,
And more of Adam never knew.

I did my Maker's law obey,
Nor from it ever went astray.
Thousands of miles I go in fear
But seldom on the earth appear.

For a purpose wise which God
  did see,
He put a living soul in me.
A soul from me my God did
  claim,
And took from me that soul
  again.

And when from me that soul
  had fled,
I was the same as when first
  made.
And without hands or feet or
  soul
I travel on from pole to pole.

I labor hard by day and night,
To fallen man I give great
  light.
Thousands of people young and
  old
Will by my death great light
  behold.

Nor right nor wrong can I
  conceive,
The Scriptures I cannot believe.
Although my name is therein
  found
They are to me an empty
  sound.

No fear of death doth trouble
  me,
Real happiness I never shall see.
To Heaven I shall never go,
Or to the grave or Hell below.

Now when these lines you
  slowly read,
Go search your Bible, with all
  speed.

For that my name's recorded there,      I honestly to you declare.

**(Solution on page 86)**

# THE ANSWERS

Introduction: Out of several hundred puzzles collected in the past fifty years these are the ones I have not been able to find published anywhere. They are the type of puzzle that makes its appearance in the form of copied sheets in offices, stores, schools and clubs. It would be after all these years almost impossible to find the origin of each one. They are assembled for your pleasure and are not all nonsensical, but touch on mathematics, history, geography, English, logic, and Bible knowledge. See how many you can solve without referring to the back answer pages, but be careful, as some may be purposely tricky and misleading to you, but very often are also most informative.

**164.** 520

**207.** While Shepherds Watched Their Flock

**32.**

| | | |
|---|---|---|
| nose | hair | neck |
| vein | skin | heel |
| palm | brow | calf |
| nail | bone | pore |
| drum | jowl | iris |
| head | chin | face |
| cell | arch | nape |
| anus | lung | knee |
| lobe | back | uvea |
| fist | lash | axon |

**34.** Polo pony. (You ride it when you play polo!)

**245.** 674 x 676 length and width would give the most square footage.

**65.** resting
feasting
dusting
jesting
roasting
rusting
interesting
fasting
tasting
toasting

**221.** I shot a squirrel in a tree. (killed)
A long shot in betting. (odds)
A shot in the arm. (vaccination)
A shot in the dark. (guessing)
A shot of liquor. (portion)
I'm all shot today. (tired)
Shot the day. (wasted)
Shot a picture. (took)
Took a shot at farming. (chance)
Shot a gun. (fired)
Shot an arrow. (expelled from a bow)
Shot a game of pool. (played)
Basketball shot. (throw)
Business is shot. (ruined)
You look shot. (bad)
Shot the works. (spent)
Shot pellets in a gun. (metal particles)
I took a shot at it. (try)
He's a big shot at work. (top man)
The bird shot out of the tree. (flew)

**90.** 10 Commandments

**198.** Jingle Bells

**250.** There is no such thing as "the world's largest number," because if anyone claimed to invent it, you would simply have to add "one" and make it a larger number. Professor Edward Krasner of Columbia University coined the GOO-

GOL, followed by the GOOGOLPLEX. To imagine the immensity of these numbers, a trillion is a number followed by 12 zeros but a GOOGOL is a number followed by 100 zeros. A GOOGOLPLEX is a GOOGOL to the GOOGOL power, or GOOGOL$^{\text{googol}}$. If the GOOGOLPLEX could be written on a single line of a typewriter, the line would be longer than ten times around the world, or farther than the distance of the earth to the moon. Even a number like GOOGOLPLEX$^{\text{googol}}$, which is beyond comprehension for man, is still not an infinite number. Gives you something to think about, doesn't it?

**91.** 1,001 Arabian Nights

**215.** Chestnuts Roasting on an Open Fire

**66.**

| 1 | 11 | 6 | 16 |
|---|----|---|----|
| 8 | 14 | 3 | 9 |
| 15 | 5 | 12 | 2 |
| 10 | 4 | 13 | 7 |

**33.** 10,096; 10,098; 10,100

**231.** Shuffle the cards until you get a chance to see what the bottom card is. Let's say the bottom card is the Jack of Spades. Spread cards on the table face down and remember where you put the Jack of Spades, even if it is partially covered with some of the other cards. When your friend picks up a card, he does not look at it but gives it to you face down. You call it the Jack of Spades, have it written down, and then you alone look at it. Let's say the card you look at is the Two of Clubs. The next card he picks up you call the Two of Clubs, have it written down, take a peek at it, and let him pick another card with the same procedure. After he has taken three or four cards, it is now your turn. You pick up that Jack of Spades you had planted and call out the last card your friend gave you before you even turn it over or look at it. Turn over all the called cards at the same time and let your friends check with the written answers. They will be amazed and baffled! Practise this a few times before you try it on someone.

**214.** We Wish You a Merry Christmas

**1.** Two apples, of course.

**92.** 12 Signs of the Zodiac

**242.** Let's call the starting point A; B, C, and D are intermediate points; and E, the shrine. Two men leave A, go out 2½ days to B, each leave 5 gallons of water, and return to A. The third man leaves A, goes to B, picks up one can, travels on to C, leaves 5 gallons of water, returns to B, picks up a 2½ gallon can of water to return back to A. Now the fourth man leaves A, goes to B, takes one can, goes on to C, and picks up a can there. He now can travel to E and back to C, take the last can left there, return to B and take the last can left *there*, to get safely back with the loot!

**64.** 2, 2, 4
7
13

**172.** Brands A and B are of equal value and C is better than either of them.

**129.** 7 Dwarfs

**71.** Take one bill from the envelope marked $15 (which is a wrong marking). Say it would be a $5 bill. Now you know the other left in the envelope is also a $5 bill. You also know now that the envelope labelled $20, since it is labelled wrong, cannot contain $20. You already know which is the correct $10 envelope, hence the one labelled $20 has to contain $15. The remaining envelope has to be the one with $20 in it. Use the same procedure if you should pick the one with the two $10 bills in it.

**46.** Several balloons were filled with helium and guided with lines from the ground. The hay wagon was made as light as possible. When the wagon was directly over the chimney, the balloons were punctured from the ground, or unhooked from the wagon from the ground and released.

Using the formula to determine the volume of a sphere $4/3\pi R3$, a six-foot weather balloon with a radius of 3 feet would be approximately 112 cubic feet. Assuming a cubic foot of helium would lift 3oz. with proper temperature and atmospheric pressure, each balloon would lift about 21 lbs. (I have a 4x4 wagon. Shipping weight was 55 lbs.)

**15.** Anything other than the words "your name" is wrong.

**94.** 9 Planets in the Solar System

**31.** Miami, United States
Mexico City, Mexico
Milan, Italy
Moscow, Russia
Melbourne, Australia
Manila, Philippines
Madrid, Spain
Manchester, England
Montreal, Canada
Montevideo, Uruguay
Madras, India
Medellín, Colombia
Marseilles, France
Munich, Germany

**93.** 54 Cards in a Deck (with the Jokers)

**199.** O Little Town of Bethlehem

**106.** 64 Squares on a Checkerboard

**248.** His pay would be about $55,214

**217.**

| B | C | D | F | G |
|---|---|---|---|---|
| N | A | P | U | R |
| W | Y | E | Q | Z |
| S | O | T | I | V |
| H | J | K | L | M |

ANY    AD    AYE    ANYWAY
AWN    AN    AWAY    DAY
APE

DUG    PAD    EYE
DUE    RUE    FUR
DUET    SOY    GURU
DUPE    SOWN    HOT
HOW    SO    IT
JOY    WAN    JOT
KET    SHOE    KITE
KILT    TO    LIE
SHOW    TOT    MILK
PUP    TOY    NAPE
BAN    TOW    OWN
BANANA    TOE    PAWN
BAY    TIE    QUE
BAD    TILT    RUG
CAN    TYPE    SOW
CAB    VIE    TOWN
CAD    SWAN    UP
CAP    SOT    VIM
CAPE    WOK    WAY
CAY    WOE    YAWN
CABANA    WAD    ZITI
LIT    YET    PUB
MIL    TEA    PUPA
MITE    TOTE    BANYAN
NAY    PAW    CAW
NAP    PETITE    CANADA
SWAY    SWAP    DAD
SHOT    SWAB    DAB
NAB    BANC    DID
PAN    CANAPE    QUEAN
PAY    DAWN    QUEUE
PET

**107.** 40 Days and Nights of the Great Flood

**171.** Brain
Cheek
Heart
Liver
Elbow
Wrist
Thumb
Tooth
Scalp
Chest
Navel
Groin
Thigh
Blood
Femur
Ankle
Pupil
Nerve
Aorta
Sinus
Trunk
Skull
Mouth
Flesh
Anvil
Uvula
Joint
Gland

**30.** 40,320 ways.
1 x 2 x 3 x 4 = 24
1 x 2 x 3 x 4 x 5 x 6 x 7 x 8 = 40,320

**244.** He sold 52 bushels of wheat, 55 bushels of corn, and 34 bushels of oats.

**19.** Translation:
"Have you any ham?"
"Yes, we have ham."
"Have you any eggs?"
"Yes, we have eggs."
"OK, ham and eggs."

**69.** Clare
Matt
Jim
Dick
Hy
Hal
Chris
Sally
Dinah

**174.** First cut the cheese in half (like a layer cake). Now cut it in four equal pieces from the top. Take three of the four quarters, which are already cut in half, stack them on top of the fourth quarter, and make your fourth cut, making 16 pieces.

**2.** Moses? Noah was the captain of the Ark.

**108.** 6 Wives of Henry the Eighth

**35.**
| | | | |
|---|---|---|---|
| 1 | 9 | 2 | 10 |
| 3 | 11 | 4 | 12 |
| 5 | 13 | 6 | 14 |
| 7 | 15 | 8 | 16 |

**230.**

| | | |
|---|---|---|
| England | Italy | Monaco |
| Spain | Ireland | Denmark |
| Greece | Italy | France |
| France | Germany | Egypt |
| Italy | Russia | Austria |
| England | Switzerland | Denmark |
| England | | |

**44.** 3,121 peanuts

| Original Bag | Monkey's Share | Purloined Portion |
|---|---|---|
| 3121 | 1 | 624 kept by #1 |
| 2496 | 1 | 499 kept by #2 |
| 1996 | 1 | 399 kept by #3 |
| 1596 | 1 | 319 kept by #4 |
| 1276 | 1 | 257 kept by #5 |
| 1020 | 1 | 204 divided among all |

**70.** chest
calves
muscle
feet
temples
pupils
heel
nails
lashes
arms

**144.** The middle spot on the dice is the "rose," so therefore the "petals" are the spots around the rose. 3 is 2 petals and 5 is 4 petals. 1, of course, is the rose. It sounds simple, but very few people can break the code.

**52.** A bit over 5½ minutes

**116.** 2 Turtle Doves (and a Partridge in a Pear Tree)

**45.** 15,621 peanuts

| Original Bag | Monkey's Share | Purloined Portion |
| --- | --- | --- |
| 15,621 | 1 | 3,124 kept by #1 |
| 12,496 | 1 | 2,499 kept by #2 |
| 9,996 | 1 | 1,999 kept by #3 |
| 7,996 | 1 | 1,599 kept by #4 |
| 6,396 | 1 | 1,279 kept by #5 |
| 5,116 | | 1,023 divided among all |

**68.** None. They would all fly away.

**241.** $1.25 to break even
$4.38 to make $25,000.00

**4.** Gus had ten pigs, Joe had fourteen pigs.

**173.** Sam would still win. He would run the extra ten yards in less time than Jake.

**54.** Her father

**137.** PFIGJLNMEKP

**81.** People who live in glass houses should not throw stones.

**115.** 1 Day at a Time

**159.** 8 4 6 2

**229.** 16 grandsons $256
13 granddaughters $169
4 great-grandchildren $16

**5.** All twelve months have 28 days.

**18.** Translation:
"Say, Willie, there they go,
Thousand buses in a row."
"No, Joe, them is trucks,
Some with cows in,
Some with ducks."

**200.** Silent Night

**190.** Divided by 6, divided by 5, times 4, times 3, divided by 2, divided by 1, equals 6
Plus 0, plus 0, minus 3, plus 0, plus 0, minus 3 = 1

**51.** UNDERGROUND

**189.** International Nickel Co. stack in New Jersey is 1,251 ft.

**47.** Five queens

**138.** 12 Letters

**251.** Jonah's whale

**26.** Seven. He makes six cigarettes, smokes them, and has six butts to make the seventh cigarette.

**14.** Whoever heard of a Mama Bull?

**149.** Shrove Tuesday, the day before Ash Wednesday, or the beginning of Lent

**227.** He is just not going to be on time this morning.

**80.** Too many cooks spoil the broth.

**170.** 40 years old

**201.** We Three Kings of Orient Are

**103.** 1 Wheel on a Unicycle

**121.** 360 Degrees in a Circle

**6.** No, he would be dead!

**117.** 4 Horsemen of the Apocalypse

**67.** Holland

**148.** Dice.

**43.** BITE
BITE
BITE
BITE

**220.** Slippery got 479 votes, Pete 471, Looie 403, and Doug 295.

**175.** E is made of four straight lines.

**240.** 20 shares @ 202  = 4,040.00
10 shares @ 13   =   130.00
50 shares @ 46¼ = 2,312.50
25 shares @ 97½ = 2,437.50
10 shares @ 108  = 1,080.00
               10,000.00

**55.** Two minutes to two to two minutes after two.
Two minutes to two to two minutes after two, too.

**36.** 80 minutes

**128.** 3 Wise Men

**139.** Use Roman numerals XIX.

**7.** One hour—for instance, if you swallowed one at 7:00, one at 7:30, and one at 8:00.

**118.** 13 Cards in a Suit

**37.** Make a pyramid out of the six toothpicks.

**176.** 88 Apples

**216.** $7,500; 10 years

**238.** 7½% to 8%

**3.** One trillion and one.

**146.** Korean War

**13.** If you printed and did not write the word, you are wrong.

**63.** TO THE HIDEOUT

**130.** 1,2 Button My Shoe

**143.** 6 (minus 2 plus 1, minus 3 plus 2, etc.)

**53.** PYX, a vessel used for religious services

**202.** The First Noël

**160.** 9 11 9 11 20 = 60

**82.** The early bird catches the worm.

**20.** About 18,000,000 miles!

**140.** 1st man sold 3 @ \$1, 30 @ 3/\$1.00 = \$13
2nd man sold 5 @ \$1, 24 @ 3/\$1.00 = \$13
3rd man sold 6 @ \$1, 21 @ 3/\$1.00 = \$13

**16.** ONE WORD

**219.** Since the earth rotates from west to east, the plane would have to fly farther to get to New York.

**114.** 30 Days Hath September, April, June, and November

**29.** The man who walked into the restaurant was a sailor who had been shipwrecked with his best buddy and another man for a month. One morning, the other man said that the best buddy had left during the night to go for help. The man then fed the sailor what he called "albatross soup" for a whole month.

**127.** 100 Legs on a Centipede

**145.** 120 holes

**209.** Away in a Manger

**131.** 206 Bones in the Body

**177.** 2½ minutes

**42.** There is at least an inch of dirt under the chair a person is sitting on (it may be under the floorboards, but it's there).

**12.** A chair, a bed, and a toothbrush.

**102.** 24 Hours in a Day

**62.** If you said 19, chalk one on your score. Your eyes are good!

**239.** He butchered three pigs on Monday morning and three in the afternoon. The rest of the week he butchered three a day. There was an odd number each time.

**188.** $10,285.33

**211.** Winter Wonderland

**157.** $0.20

**73.** Jack and Jill

**48.** Over 3,000 miles long

**228.** 7 days

**247.** 5,050

**179.** Between 10 and 3. The numbers are written alphabetically.

**86.** An ill wind blows no good.

**109.** 101 Dalmatians

**225.** SOMERSAULT

**95.** 88 Piano Keys

**197.** Deck the Halls

**165.** B

**213.** Frostie the Snowman

**246.** xyz goes below the line because above the line is the entire Hawaiian alphabet!

**119.** 8 Parts of Speech in the English Language

**21.** Over a million dollars

**141.** First day sales were 2 subscriptions, then 5, 8, 11, 14, 17, 20, 23, which total 100.

**187.** $4,250.00

**61.** Peacocks do not lay eggs. Peahens do!

**233.**

```
    5  8  3
  + 1  4  6
  ─────────
    7  2  9
```

**191.** Come All Ye Faithful

**151.** Bookkeeper

**79.** A rolling stone gathers no moss.

**226.**

```
  9  5  7      4  3  6      6  5  4  2
     5  2  8      5  6  4      2  4  5  6
  ─────────   ─────────   ────────────
  1  4  8  5   1  0  0  0   8  9  9  8
```

**168.** Camel

**142.** 58 (times 2 plus 3)

**120.** 20,000 Leagues Under the Sea

**23.** Both would be the same distance from City A.

**182.** 8 (plus 1 times 2, plus 1 times 2, etc.)

**237.** 43 are the numbers for SO

**152.** 1 Horsepower

**41.** 43

**11.** 12,111.

**101.** 3 Blind Mice (See How They Run)

**56.** 8 will have 3 black faces
24 will have 2 black faces
24 will have 1 black face
8 will be white

**132.** 6 Sides on a Hexagon

**192.** Joy to the World

**78.** Three Blind Mice

**208.** What Child Is This?

**232.** Thirteen cans on the bottom row to one on top, but he would have to have four cans deep to use all 720.

**193.** Hark, the Herald Angels Sing

**40.** Two out of a set of triplets

**50.** Over 55 feet

**126.** 32 Teeth including Wisdom Teeth

**104.** 1,000 Words that a Picture Is Worth

**87.** Twinkle, Twinkle, Little Star

**113.** 40 Thieves with Ali Baba

**125.** 6 Sides on a Cube

**222.** The day that they turn the clocks back when Daylight Savings Time is over has 25 hours!

**25.** They were both women's teams.

**194.** God Rest Ye Merry Gentlemen

**161.** 7 7 7 5 = 26
7 7 5 10 = 29

**100.** 8 Sides on a Stop Sign

**136.** 4 Cylinders in a Compact Car

**49.** Jim's average is higher.

**77.** Jack Sprat Could Eat No Fat

**186.** 200 miles a day

**10.** Approximately 3.2 years to count to a mere billion, and about 3,200 years to count to a trillion.

**218.** 17,16,15,14,13,12,11,10,9. Actually, nine trips are made in the 8 days.

**181.** I. (A skip 2 letters, D skip 2 letters, etc.)

**60.** 48 miles per hour. Let us say the distance was 60 miles (120 miles round trip). Travelling 60 m.p.h. it would take 60 minutes. Travelling 40 m.p.h. it would take 90 minutes. Total 150 minutes or 2½ hours. Averaging a speed of 48 m.p.h. for 2½ hours, you would cover 120 miles.

**22.** Approximately $775,000.

**156.** Mary

**169.** 100% of the people drank liquor.

**99.** 200 Dollars for Passing "Go" in Monopoly

**88.** 26 Letters of the Alphabet

**162.** 15  15  17  17  18  18 = 100

**203.** I'm Dreaming of a White Christmas

**8.** Friday

**83.** All that glitters is not gold.

**39.** 58 seconds

**235.** 3% is more.

**163.** 1/1/01 (2001)

**212.** Go Tell It on the Mountain

**17.** $500 every six months is better. To prove it, take a $10,000 a year salary: $500 every six months; $2,000 per year

| 1st year: | $5,000 + $5,500 = $10,500 | *vs* | $10,000 |
| 2nd year: | $6,000 + $6,500 = $12,500 | *vs* | $12,000 |
| 3rd year: | $7,000 + $7,500 = $14,500 | *vs* | $14,000 |

**155.** Leo times Taurus minus Pisces divided by Cancer times Gemini = 12

**59.** Ten of Diamonds, King of Hearts, and Eight of Spades

**76.** Mary, Mary, Quite Contrary

**178.** It would be 5:46, or 14 minutes to 6

**135.** 21 Gun Salute

**195.** O Holy Night

**204.** Rudolph, the Rednose Reindeer

**223.** 80 ft. wide

**124.** 2001: A Space Odyssey

**24.** House numbers!

**105.** 29 Days in February in a Leap Year

**89.** 7 Wonders of the Ancient World

**185.** 2,521

**112.** 5 Fingers on Each Hand (or Toes on Each Foot)

**150.** Slightly under 64% A, 25% B

**133.** 4 Seasons in a Year

**72.** Mary Had a Little Lamb

**58.** 16 spaces

**98.** 90 Degrees in a Right Angle

**205.** The Little Drummer Boy

**184.** 3 hours, 45 minutes

**9.** The second day of the week is pronounced Mon-day!

**74.** Little Jack Horner

**28.** A baseball player.

**154.** Hong Kong

**134.** 2 Years before the Mast

**57.** GH in ENOUGH sounds like F
O in WOMEN sounds like I (wimmen)
TI in NOTION sounds like SH

**123.** 13 Baker's Dozen

**167.** 101 chickens

**38.** "What"

**234.** 35,000 miles

**84.** Haste makes waste.


**97.** 18 Holes in a Golf Course

**206.** O Christmas Tree

**166.** $26^3 \times 10^3 = 17,576,000$
$26 \times 25 \times 24 \times 10 \times 9 \times 8 = 11,232,000$

**122.** 60 Minutes in an Hour

**153.** Red

**85.** A fool and his money are soon parted.

**196.** It Came upon a Midnight Clear

**27.** He had hiccoughs!

**75.** Old Mother Hubbard

**180.** 16

**224.** 50 ft. approximately

**243.** I got as far as 31 years and still had around $10 equity left.

**96.** 32 Degrees Fahrenheit, at which Water Freezes

**110.** 60 Seconds in a Minute

**210.** Santa Claus Is Coming to Town

**147.** Penguin

**111.** Seven Hills of Rome

**249.** 320 m.p.h.; 400 m.p.h.

**233.**

```
    5   8   3
 +1   4   6
 ─────────────
    7   2   9
```

**236.** 15   31   7   15   23

**183.**

| Start–7——— | 9⌐ | 13 |
|---|---|---|
| 3 | 5 ⌐—7⌐ | 15 |
| 16 | 4 ⌐ 7 ⌐——11⌐ |
| 15 | 1 ⌐—3⌐ | Finish |

**158.**

# Index